# 50

## fantastic ideas for
## seasons

ALISTAIR BRYCE-CLEGG

Featherstone
An imprint of Bloomsbury Publishing Plc

50 Bedford Square
London
WC1B 3DP
UK

1385 Broadway
New York
NY 10018
USA

www.bloomsbury.com

Bloomsbury is a registered trademark of Bloomsbury Publishing Plc

First published 2015

© Alistair Bryce-Clegg, 2015

Photographs © Fee Bryce-Clegg/ © Shutterstock.

British Library Cataloguing-in-Publication Data
A catalogue record for this book is available from the British Library.

ISBN:
PB 978-1-4729-1326-5
ePDF 978-1-4729-2474-2

Library of Congress Cataloging-in-Publication Data
A catalogue record for this book is available from the Library of Congress.

10 9 8 7 6 5 4 3 2 1

Printed and bound in India by Replika Press Pvt. Ltd.

This book is produced using paper that is made from wood grown in managed, sustainable forests. It is natural, renewable and recyclable. The logging and manufacturing processes conform to the environmental regulations of the country of origin.

To view more of our titles please visit www.bloomsbury.com

# Contents

# Introduction

There are lots of things in life that you cannot guarantee, but we all know that the seasons will come around every year and always in the same order! Although the weather may not always be what we would ideally like - or be expecting - there are lots of activities that we can plan and do to support children's growing knowledge and experience of each season, as well as utilise some of the 'typical' resources that are available.

In **50 Fantastic Ideas for Seasons** I have collected together lots of ideas that have been used to engage children and help them to recognise the distinguishing signs of each season as well as have some fun!

Although the activities in this book have been grouped by season, lots of them will be interchangeable and can be used throughout the year with just a quick tweak of some of the resources. There is a good mix of indoor and outdoor experiences that have been specifically chosen to develop a wide range of skills.

Even though when we are planning an activity we imagine what the outcome will be, it is important to let the children experience and explore the resources provided and interpret them in their own way - they are often full of surprises!

## Activity format

All the activities in this series follow the same structure. Starting with 'What you need' which lists the resources required for the activity - the majority are basic resources that are likely to be found already in most settings. It is recommended that you check the 'What you need' list well before embarking on any activity with the children, as well as reading through what the items are needed for. 'Top tip' boxes don't feature in every activity but where appropriate offer a brief suggestion, warning or piece of advice to help in tackling the activity. 'What to do' gives step-by-step instructions for completing the tasks. You should read through the instructions before you start the activity with the children, to ensure you are clear about everything. 'Taking it forward' contains further ideas for additional activities on the same theme. They have been designed to extend the children's experience and broaden their skills. Finally, 'What's in it for the children?' is a brief statement which indicates how the activities contribute to children's learning and development.

## Food allergy alert

When using food produce to enhance your play opportunities, always be mindful of potential food allergies. Look out for this symbol on the relevant pages.

## Skin allergy alert

Some detergents and soaps can cause skin reactions. Always be aware of potential skin allergies when letting children mix materials with their hands, and always provide facilities for children to wash their hands afterwards. Watch out for this symbol on the relevant pages.

## Safety issues

Children may need help and to be reminded to wash their hands when using natural materials or preparing food. They may also need reminding not to put things in their mouths, and to be told to be extra careful with real-life or found resources.

# Terrarium

## What you need:

- **Any clear plastic containers** (aquarium, sweet jars, drinks bottles with the top half cut off)
- **Pea gravel**
- **Potting compost**
- **Selection of plants**
- **Scissors**
- **Tape**
- **Accessories** (such as small models, action figures, anything you like!)

## What to do:

1. Talk about how plants come to life and start to grow in spring. Explain that you are going to make a special growing chamber to encourage small plants to grow.

2. Put a layer of gravel in the bottom of the container (for small containers about 1 cm, for large containers about 3 cm).

3. Fill the container up to a third to half full of moist potting compost.

4. Add the plants, placing the tallest at the back and the smallest at the front. Talk to the children about why you might position them this way.

5. Add any extra accessories to the container to personalise your terrarium.

6. Place the completed terrarium on a windowsill in indirect sunlight and remember to water.

### Taking it forward

- You can create one large terrarium or let the children make individual ones using smaller containers.

- You can make a seed terrarium by replacing the plants with seeds and watching them grow.

### What's in it for the children?

The children will have lots of opportunities to learn about how plants grow and what they need to survive and flourish.

### Top tip

Ask parents to contribute small plants or cuttings to fill the terrariums.

# Green fingers!

## What you need:

- Latex gloves
- Teaspoon
- Compost
- Seeds (various)
- Water

## What to do:

1. Turn back the opening to the end of the glove to make the finger holes easier to access.

2. Fill the thumb and each finger with compost using the teaspoon.

3. Press a small number of different types of seeds into each finger.

4. Carefully sprinkle each finger with a small amount of water.

5. Hang the filled glove in a warm, bright place and watch the seeds grow.

### Taking it forward

- If you want quick results, use seeds like cress or mustard.

- This activity also works really well with beans!

### What's in it for the children?

The individual glove fingers will help the children to see how different plants and seeds grow at different rates even though they all need the same conditions to survive.

# Rainbow seeds

## What you need:

- Teaspoon
- Basil seeds
- Seven paper cups or containers
- Hot water
- Food colouring or liquid water colour, preferably in the colours of the rainbow

## What to do:

1. Put a teaspoon of basil seeds into each of the seven cups or containers.
2. Half fill each of the cups or containers with hot water.
3. Add a few drops of food colouring or liquid water colour to each cup or container (ideally a different rainbow colour in each one).
4. Leave the container for three or four hours so the food colouring can soak in well.
5. Drain any excess water.
6. Pour out and allow the children to play with the mixture. The play is open ended and will engage multiple senses.

### Taking it forward

- You can use these basil seed containers as enhancements to a number of areas of learning e.g. use some magnifying glasses for observing the basil seeds up close.
- Give the children some tweezers and ask them to see how many basil seeds they can 'catch'.
- Of course, you can always try growing them!

### What's in it for the children?

The children will see the seeds change from tiny black dots to small balls of colour. This is because the seeds will absorb the moisture and hold onto it to help them grow. This should give you lots to talk to the children about.

### Top tip

If after you have soaked the seeds they look too pale, add a little more food colouring.

### ➕ Health & Safety

Make sure an adult pours the hot water to avoid spills and burns.

# Butterfly sensory bag

## What you need:

- Small freezer bags (zip lock)
- Ready mixed paint or hair gel
- Glitter and sequins (optional)
- Pipe cleaners or wooden pegs

## What to do:

1. Fill a freezer bag a third full with paint or hair gel.
2. Add sequins or glitter.
3. Close the bag (squeezing any air out as you do).
4. Squish the bag a bit to distribute the paint.
5. Flatten the bag.
6. Squeeze the opposite sides of the bag together until they meet in the middle.
7. Wrap your pipe cleaner around the middle of your bag, (or use a wooden peg) leaving two long ends for the butterfly's antennae.

### Taking it forward

Try using different sized freezer bags to make a range of butterflies in a range of sizes.

### What's in it for the children?

This is a great activity for children to explore their sense of sight, touch and smell (if you use the hair gel). It also involves some fine motor manipulation skills when wrapping the pipe cleaner around the middle of the bag.

# Recycled bird feeder

## What you need:

- Small milk carton
- Ruler
- Scissors
- Hole punch
- String
- Birdseed
- Objects for decoration

## What to do:

1. Talk to the children about feeding the birds in spring by providing bird feeders in the trees. Explain that you are going to recycle some containers to help feed the birds.

2. Begin by taking one corner of the carton, measure 5 cm up from the bottom and then mark.

3. From the mark you just made, measure 5 cm across the flat side to the right and the flat side to the left and draw a line.

4. At the end of each line that you have just made, draw a straight line down to the bottom of your carton.

5. Using a sharp pair of scissors **(adult)**, cut along the lines that you have drawn.

6. Cut around the edge of the base, leaving the full base in tact.

7. At this point, you might want to decorate the milk carton.

8. If you are using a cardboard carton, punch a hole in the top of the carton. Thread a string through the hole, so you can hang the feeder outside.

9. If you are using a plastic carton, make a hole in the centre of the lid and thread a piece of string through it, knotting it well underneath the lid. Then, screw the lid back in place.

10. Fill your bird feeders with seed and then hang outside.

11. Watch as different birds visit the feeders.

Taking it forward

■ Children can make multiple bird feeders and try different seeds and treats to see which ones are most popular with the birds.

What's in it for the children?

Making and watching the birds use the feeder helps the children to understand about how animals are different from humans, how they live, what they eat and what they need to survive.

Glue Stick

# Spring flowers on a light box

## What you need:

- Plastic box
- Fairy lights
- Strong tape
- Perspex or a plastic sheet the same size as the top of your box

## What to do:

1. Fill your plastic box with fairy lights (leaving enough wire loose to allow you to plug them in).

2. Tape the Perspex or plastic to the top of the box.

3. Turn on the fairy lights. You have now created a 'light box'!

4. Position an assortment of spring flowers on top of your 'light box', and let the children observe them. Encourage children to study the different textures and patterns of the petals and leaves.

### Taking it forward

- Use whiteboard markers to draw or write on your plastic sheet – you may wish to annotate the different parts of the flowers.

- Provide magnifying glasses for the children so they can observe the flowers more closely.

- Add paper, pencils and pens to encourage the children to draw and write about what they see.

### What's in it for the children?

This activity gives the children an opportunity to observe flowers, leaves and petals closely. The light that shines from underneath will allow the children to view what they are looking at in a different way to their usual day-to-day observation. This is also a great activity to encourage talk and mark making.

# Flower printing

## What you need:

- Various spring flowers
- Pegs
- Paint in spring colours
- Trays or containers
- Paper

## What to do:

1. Cut the heads off the flowers, leaving a short amount of stem.
2. Attach a peg to each flower head by the stem so they are easy to pick up.
3. Pour some paint into the trays or containers.
4. Dip the flower heads into the trays.
5. Carefully print with the flower heads onto paper (as shown in the picture below).

### Taking it forward

- Don't just save this activity for spring, do it all year round using the flowers that are in season.
- Link to colour mixing by encouraging the children to mix paint that matches the colour of the flower that they are printing with.

### What's in it for the children?

This is a good opportunity for the children to build and consolidate their knowledge of flowers and plants that grow in the spring.

# Leaf hammering

## What you need:

- Green leaves
- Flowers and petals
- Herbs
- **Two squares of calico, cotton or kitchen towel** (light colours are best)
- Small hammer

## What to do:

1. Lay out the selection of leaves, flowers and herbs on one piece of fabric.
2. Place the other piece of fabric directly on top, so that it covers the first.
3. Carefully hammer over the top of the cloth.
4. Keep hammering until you can see the clear outline of the object underneath.
5. Remove the leaves, flowers and herbs and admire your art work!

### Taking it forward

- This activity can be done on a large scale with a number of children working on one piece or on an individual basis with one child using one leaf or flower to create their own piece.

- Arrange your leaves and petals into a pattern before you start hammering.

### What's in it for the children?

This activity will give the children an opportunity to observe the leaves, petals, flowers etc closely. There will also be lots of opportunities for children to talk about how and why the colour comes out of the plants and into the fabric.

### Health & Safety

Show the children how to use the hammer carefully. Explain that tools must be respected and used carefully for specific tasks.

# Clouds in a jar

## What you need:

- Jam jar
- Shaving foam
- Pipette or dropper
- Food colouring or liquid water colour
- Water

## What to do:

1. Fill two thirds of the jar with water.
2. Squirt shaving foam onto the water.
3. Use the pipette or dropper to drip food colouring onto the top of the foam.
4. Watch as the colour sinks into the foam and then emerges from the other side, like drops of rain from a cloud.
5. Add more colour until the water is no longer clear.

### Taking it forward

- Try this on a larger scale in a vase or water tray.
- Use specific colours for colour mixing.

### What's in it for the children?

There are lots of opportunities for talk about weather in this activity. Children will also have the opportunity to think about clouds and what happens when it rains.

# Make a rain stick

## What you need:

- Kitchen roll tube
- Split pins
- Cardboard
- Pencil
- Scissors
- Masking tape
- Paint
- Paper
- Glue
- Decoration
- Lentils

## What to do:

1. Place the kitchen roll tube on to the cardboard and draw around it. Repeat this in several places.
2. Cut out two of the circles.
3. Attach one circle to one end of the tube using tape.
4. Put two tablespoons of lentils into the tube.
5. Attach the other circle to the other end of the tube and secure it with tape.
6. Use the paint and paper to decorate your rain stick and then leave it to dry.
7. Push the split pins into your rain stick. This can be completely at random or in a pattern.
8. How many split pins you use is up to you. The lentils will bounce off them as they fall through the tube, making a better sound.

## Top tip ⭐

If children struggle to push the split pins through the tube, let an adult make a 'pilot' hole first with the end of a sharp pencil or some scissors.

### Taking it forward

- You can make huge rain sticks from packaging tubes and substitute the lentils for split peas or chick peas.

### What's in it for the children?

The process of making this activity is great for developing children's fine motor dexterity. When they have made their rain sticks encourage them to use their listening skills and make comparisons.

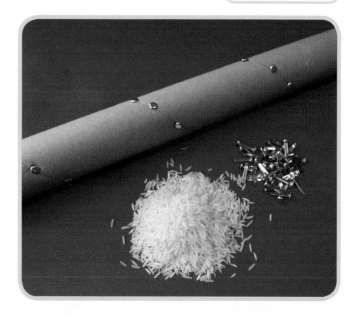

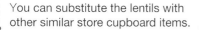

### Top tip ⭐

You can substitute the lentils with other similar store cupboard items.

# Puddle painting

## What you need:

- Small containers
- Food colouring
- Oil
- Spoon
- Paper
- A puddle!

## What to do:

1. Pour enough oil into each of your containers to cover the bottom.

2. Add a few drops of food colouring to each container (one colour per container).

3. Stir well until the colour separates within the oil.

4. Find a puddle.

5. Pour the contents of your containers onto the surface of the puddle.

6. Lay a piece of paper on top of the puddle.

7. Wait for around five seconds and then remove the paper.

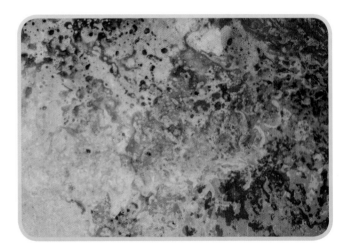

### Taking it forward

- This activity works equally as well on wet tarmac, paving stones or rubberised playground surfaces.

### What's in it for the children?

This is a great opportunity for some outdoor creativity exploration. There are also lots of opportunities to talk about how the oily paint floats on the water.

### Top tip ★

Don't wait too long after pouring out the contents of your pots before putting down the paper – otherwise you might find all of your colour has sunk to the bottom of your puddle!

# 3D rain paint

## What you need:

- PVA glue
- Water
- Blue paint, food colouring or liquid water colour
- Card or paper
- Syringe
- Pot or container

## What to do:

1. In your container, mix one part PVA with one part water.
2. Add colour until you get your ideal colour for rain!
3. Prop up the card or paper so that it is at a slight angle.
4. Fill your syringe with the PVA and water mix.
5. Slowly squirt the PVA mix in a line across the top of the paper.
6. Watch it work its way down the paper in a thick drips.
7. Add more PVA to the top of the paper if necessary.
8. Leave to dry.

### Taking it forward

- Once dry ask the children to draw or paint their own rainy day picture in the space underneath the drips.
- Add glitter to your PVA for sparkly rain (like in the picture below).

### What's in it for the children?

The children will be able to observe change within a material and its properties. They will also be able to talk about the movement of the liquid, and their own experiences of rain and rainy days.

# Marshmallow shooter

## What you need:

- 30 cm of 1.25 cm waste pipe
- Mini marshmallows
- One 1.25 cm end cap
- Two 1.25 cm elbow joint
- One 1.25 cm 'T' joint
- Junior hacksaw

## What to do:

1. Cut the 30 cm of pipe into two 7 cm and three 5 cm pieces.
2. Slot together using the elbow joints and end cap.
3. Blow a marshmallow down the mouthpiece and watch it fly!

### Taking it forward

- Create targets for the children to aim at.
- Make different sized shooters using larger pipes, and joints.

### What's in it for the children?

There will be a high level of engagement from this sunny day activity. The children not only get to use real tools, but also their construction skills, as well as hand-eye coordination and aim.

### Health & Safety

Make sure an adult supervises use of the hacksaw. Ensure that all risk assessments have been carried out and be aware that marshmallows can present a choking hazard. Never leave the children unattended with this activity.

# Rubber glove finger puppets

## What you need:

- Rubber gloves
- Scissors
- Permanent markers

**Taking it forward**

- Add the rubber glove finger puppets to your small world provision both indoors and outdoors.

**What's in it for the children?**

These finger puppets are really easy to make and use. Because they are made from rubber gloves they also last a lot longer than paper ones. They are great for encouraging children's imagination and developing talk.

## What to do:

1. Lay the rubber gloves onto a flat surface.
2. Use the markers to draw faces onto the fingers of the gloves.
3. Cut off the fingers.
4. Create an outdoor puppet theatre for Summer puppet shows.

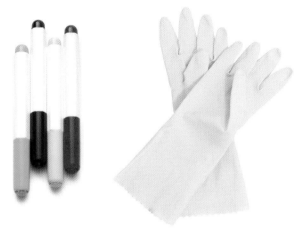

# Soap boats

## What you need:

- Paper
- Tape
- Guttering
- Water
- Small bars of soap
- Cocktail stick

## What to do:

1. Cut out a small triangle of paper.
2. Attach to a cocktail stick with tape.
3. Push the cocktail stick into the middle of a small bar of soap.
4. Prop the guttering at an angle.
5. Wet the guttering with a small amount of water (you will need to repeat this step throughout the process).
6. Let the children slide their soap boats down the guttering.

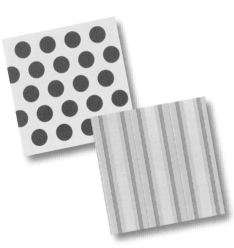

### Taking it forward

- Set up multiple lengths of guttering and let the children race their soap boats.

### What's in it for the children?

Apart from being great fun, children have the opportunity to see how the water dissolves the soap and how the soap makes the inside of the guttering slippery.

# Texture stamping in clay

## What you need:

- Air dry clay
- **Collection of resources to press into the clay** (This is a great opportunity to collect resources related to signs of summer that the children will be experiencing.)

## What to do:

1. Show the children how to take a small ball of clay and shape it into a bowl shape using their thumb and fingers.
2. Make sure that the sides of their bowls are not too thin.
3. Take one of the objects that you have collected and press it into the side or bottom of your bowl.
4. Remove the object.
5. Leave the bowl to dry.

### Taking it forward

- You can apply the same process to a flat piece of clay rather than a bowl.
- Encourage the children to paint and decorate their clay bowls once they are dry.

### What's in it for the children?

This process is not only good for developing children's fine motor dexterity, it also gives them an opportunity to experience texture and the properties of different materials.

# Bouncing bubbles

## What you need:

- A cup of distilled drinking water
- A tablespoon of washing-up liquid
- A teaspoon of glycerine
- A straw or bubble blower
- Bowl or jar
- A sock or woolly glove

## What to do:

1. Mix all of the ingredients together in the bowl or jar.
2. Leave it for 24 hours.
3. Put a sock or glove onto one hand and a straw or bubble blower in the other.
4. Dip the straw or bubble blower into the mixture.
5. Blow some bubbles.
6. Catch the bubbles on the sock or glove without them bursting.

### Top tip ⭐

You can use wire, string or pipe cleaners to make bubble blowers that produce huge bubbles.

**What's in it for the children?**

Apart from the science of creating a bubble in the first place, there are lots of opportunities for talk and questioning about how and why the bubbles don't burst.

# Shower caps and shaving foam

## What you need:

- Shower cap
- Shaving foam
- Polystyrene packing chips

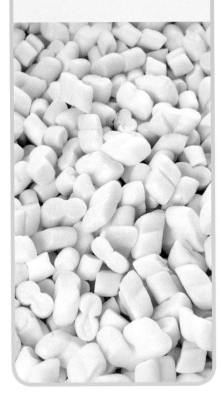

## What to do:

1. Ask one child to put on a shower cap.
2. Ask another child to cover the cap in shaving foam.
3. Invite other children to throw packing chips at the cap, trying to get them to stick.

### Taking it forward

- You can play this as a team game where a number of children wear shower caps and are 'runners' and a number of children who throw the polystyrene chips are 'chasers'.

### What's in it for the children?

This is a great Summer fun activity to get children moving. It also helps children to develop their gross motor skills as well as their hand-eye coordination, balance and dexterity.

# Frozen smoothie paints

## What you need:

- Shaving foam
- Bowl
- Ready mix or powder paint
- Ice cubes
- Hand blender

## What to do:

1. Squirt a generous amount of shaving foam into the bowl.
2. Add the paint.
3. Add five or six ice cubes.
4. Blend them all together with the hand blender (adults only) until the ice appears crushed but not completely melted.
5. Decant into smaller bowls.
6. Get painting with the smoothie mix!

### Taking it forward

- Make lots of different colours of smoothie paint by repeating the process with different colours.

### What's in it for the children?

This is a different paint experience for children. As the ice in the smoothie paint melts, the paint process keeps on changing.

### Top tip

If the smoothie paint becomes over blended, then just add more ice.

# Ice cream play dough

## What you need:

- **¾ cup of hair conditioner** (use the cheapest supermarket brand available)
- **1½ cups of cornflour**

Optional:

- **A few drops of food colouring**
- **Flavouring** (either real or essence)

## What to do:

1. Put the conditioner into the bowl.

2. If you want coloured and flavoured ice cream play dough then add the flavour and colour to the conditioner and mix well.

3. Add the cornflour slowly and keep stirring.

**Taking it forward**

- The trick with getting the dough to look like ice cream is to keep adding the cornflour a little bit at a time. If you don't add enough you will end up with goo!

**What's in it for the children?**

This dough is a great addition to children's summer role play experience. It also changes its form and texture the more that you work with it, giving the children a number of possible ways to explore texture.

# Fizzy ice

## What you need:

- Water
- Bicarbonate of soda
- Ice cube tray or mould
- Pipette or eye dropper
- Vinegar
- Food colouring (optional)

## What to do:

1. Dissolve two tablespoons of bicarbonate of soda into one cup of water.
2. Add food colouring (optional).
3. Pour into your ice cube tray or mould.
4. Freeze overnight.
5. Turn the ice out of the mould into a bowl or container.
6. Using the pipette or eye dropper, drip vinegar onto your ice.
7. Watch it fizz.

### Taking it forward

- Add different amounts of bicarbonate of soda to your water for a more concentrated fizz.
- Sprinkle the ice with bicarbonate of soda before you add the vinegar for even more fizz!

### What's in it for the children?

The children will have the opportunity to observe how some materials change their properties when the conditions around them change. Hot summer days are perfect for this. They will also observe how different substances can react with each other.

# Beach dough

## What you need:

- Two cups of play sand
- One or more cups of flour
- ½ cup of water
- Two tablespoons of vegetable oil
- Mixing bowl
- Spoon

## What to do:

1. Mix the sand and the flour together in the bowl.
2. Slowly add the water, stirring constantly.
3. Once all of the water has been combined then add the oil and mix together with your hands.
4. If the mixture is too wet, add more sand or flour. If it is too dry, add more water.
5. Once the mixture has come together and does not stick to your hands, it is ready to be played with.

**Taking it forward**

- Add some shells, driftwood or pebbles to enhance your beach dough play.

**What's in it for the children?**

This is a recipe that children can follow and create themselves. There is also lots of opportunity for talk around children's own experiences of the beach, as well as discussing the texture of the dough that they are creating.

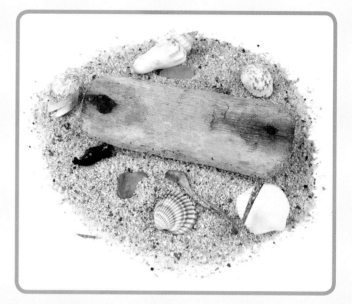

# Rubber band snap painting

## What you need:

- Baking tray
- Paper
- Elastic bands
- Metallic Paint
- Paint brush

## What to do:

1. Put a piece of paper in the bottom of a baking tray.
2. Stretch some elastic bands around the baking tray (as shown in the picture below).
3. Using a brush, paint the top of your elastic bands.
4. Flick the elastic bands to splatter the paint onto the paper below.

### Taking it forward

- Put summer flowers into the bottom of your tray and splat the paint onto them. This will add pattern to the flowers, and leave an interesting outline on your paper.

- You could use grass or twigs instead of a paint brush to create a different textural experience.

### What's in it for the children?

The children will have the opportunity to see forces at work and also explore the concept of cause and effect. They will also be learning a different way to paint.

# Rock dominoes

## What you need:

- Small pebbles
- Paintbrushes
- Masking tape
- Acrylic paint
- Spray varnish (optional)

## What to do:

1. Make sure that the pebbles are clean.
2. Put a piece of masking tape on one side of each pebble.
3. Using the acrylic paint and a brush, paint the untaped side of the pebble.
4. Paint several different pebbles in several different colours.
5. Once dry, remove the tape and repeat the process on the other side of the pebble, using a different colour.
6. Once dry, spray or paint with varnish.

### Taking it forward

- You could add dots to your coloured pebbles with a permanent marker to make them look more like traditional dominoes.
- Add pictures of insects to your dominoes for a mini-beast matching game.

### What's in it for the children?

These dominoes support children in their exploration of texture and colour. They encourage children to develop their matching skills, as well as turn taking and sharing. You can make large and small dominoes to add to your summer outdoor play provision.

# Mushroom printing

## What you need:

- Large and small mushrooms
- White paper
- Hairspray

## What to do:

1. Take the stems off the mushrooms.
2. Lay the mushrooms flat onto the paper with the top of the mushroom facing up.
3. Leave overnight.
4. Carefully remove the mushrooms from the paper by lifting rather than dragging.
5. To stop the print that has been made from smudging, spray the pictures with a light coating of hairspray.

### Taking it forward

- Try using different sized mushrooms to make different patterns.
- Experiment with different colours and textures of paper.

### What's in it for the children?

The children see nature at work as the mushroom releases its spores. This is also a good opportunity to talk to the children about why not all mushrooms are good for us and that they should never eat them without an adult's permission.

### ✚ Health & Safety

Warn children that they must not eat the mushrooms and to wash their hands after handling them.

## What you need:

- Jam jars or plastic jars
- Water
- Vegetable oil
- Food colouring or liquid water colour
- Autumn resources such as leaves, seeds, twigs etc

## What to do:

1. Half fill the jar with water and then fill to the top with oil.

2. Drop the colour into the oil.

3. Add autumn resources to your jar (but be careful not to over fill).

4. Secure the lid.

5. Move the jar around and watch how the oil and water interchange.

### Taking it forward

- You can use a large plastic sweet jar if you want to include larger resources.

- These jars are very effective on a windowsill because you can see how the light is reflected and filtered in the oil and coloured water.

### What's in it for the children?

This is a great activity for developing children's observational skills. It also gives them the opportunity to consolidate what they know about signs and features of autumn.

# Leaf stick puppets

## What you need:

- Autumn leaves
- Newspaper
- A heavy weight
- Permanent markers
- Twigs
- Tape or glue

## Top tip ★

Coating your leaves with PVA glue and allowing them to dry will help them to last longer.

## What to do:

1. Place the leaves in between two sheets of newspaper.
2. Press them under a heavy weight overnight.
3. Take your pressed leaves and draw a face onto them.
4. Attach your leaf to a stick or twig using glue or tape.
5. Create your own puppet show or act out a familiar story.

### Taking it forward

- Look for leaves that remind children of objects or animals, and create puppets with these.

### What's in it for the children?

Puppet making is not only good for developing children's creativity and skill level, but also encourages the use of talk, language and imagination.

# Sticky backed twig frame

## What you need:

- Twigs/sticks and other autumnal finds
- String
- Tape
- Sticky backed plastic

## What to do:

1. Snap or cut the sticks/twigs until they are the length that you want for the size of your frame.

2. Tie the twigs together at the corners using string.

3. Lay the frame onto the sticky backed plastic and draw around it.

4. Cut out a piece of sticky backed plastic to fit your frame.

5. Peel the backing off your sticky backed plastic. Stick it onto the back of your frame with the sticky side facing the front.

6. Secure the sticky backed plastic on the back of your frame with tape.

7. You can now stick your autumnal 'finds' into the sticky twig frame.

### Taking it forward

- Make small versions of these frames to display individual finds such as leaves or sycamore keys.

- You can also create large versions of this frame for a collective or collaborative project.

### What's in it for the children?

The creation of the frame encourages children to use their fine motor dexterity. Once made, the frame is an immediate way for children to arrange and display their autumnal finds.

# Wool wrap wigwam

## What you need:

- Large sticks/branches
- Coloured wool or twine
- String

## What to do:

1. Take the large sticks and wrap sections in coloured wool.
2. When all the sticks are complete, stand them up in a bunch.
3. Loosely bind the end of the sticks with string.
4. Spread out the base of the sticks to create a tent/wigwam shaped structure.
5. When the structure is stable, bind the top of it securely with your string.

### Taking it forward

- Make multiple structures for both indoor and outdoor play.
- Let the children replicate the process with small sticks and twigs for their small world play.

### What's in it for the children?

Binding the sticks with wool is a good challenge for children's fine motor dexterity and provides opportunities to explore colour and texture. The creation of the structure will allow children to use their construction and negotiation skills.

# Painted leaves

## What you need:

- Shallow tray or container
- Shaving foam
- Ready mixed paint
- Cocktail stick or cotton bud
- Autumn leaves

## What to do:

**1.** Cover the bottom of the tray or container with shaving foam.

**2.** Drizzle paint over the shaving foam.

**3.** Using the cocktail stick or cotton bud, swirl the paint into the foam but do not completely mix.

**4.** Lay the leaves face down into the foam.

**5.** Lift and leave to dry.

Taking it forward

- You can try this activity with leaf templates as well as real leaves.

- For really flat leaves, press them overnight before you use them between two sheets of newspaper.

What's in it for the children?

This is a lovely activity for supporting children's experience of texture and colour mixing. They will be using their fine motor dexterity in the swirling of the foam and paint, and provides lots of opportunities to talk about what they know about autumn.

# Flying conkers

## What you need:

- Conkers
- Tissue paper
- Scissors
- Glue gun or strong tape

## What to do:

1. Cut the tissue paper into long strips.
2. Gather a few strips together and attach to the bottom of a conker using a glue gun or strong tape.
3. Throw the conkers as high as you can in the air.
4. Watch the conkers fly and listen to their tails rustle in the air.

### Taking it forward

- Have competitions for who can throw their conkers the furthest.
- Give some conkers long tails and some short tails and see what difference it makes.

### What's in it for the children?

The children will be developing their gross motor dexterity as well as working on balance, hand-eye coordination and proprioception.

# Tissue paper painting

## What you need:

- Tissue paper in autumn colours
- White paper
- Paintbrushes
- Water
- Spray bottle
- Baking parchment

## What to do:

1. Cut the tissue paper into large squares.
2. Lay the squares on top of the white paper.
3. Spray the tissue paper with water until it is damp.
4. Lay a piece of baking parchment over the top of the wet tissue paper and rub with your hands.
5. Remove the baking parchment.
6. Peel off the tissue paper to reveal your artwork.

### Taking it forward

- Use different shades of paper in similar colours to produce interesting tones.
- Try cutting the tissue paper into autumn leaf shapes.

### What's in it for the children?

The children will not only be inspired by the colours of autumn to create their artwork, they also experience the effect that water has on the tissue paper, both in the way that it changes its composition and causes it to lose colour.

# Coffee filter leaves

## What you need:

- Paper coffee filters
- Pipettes or droppers
- Liquid water colour or food colouring
- Shallow tray or container
- Leaf or leaf template

## What to do:

1. Put a paper coffee filter into the bottom of a shallow tray or container.

2. Use the pipette or dropper to drop the liquid water colour or food colouring onto the filter.

3. Encourage the children to choose colours that match the autumnal leaves that they are looking at.

4. Wait until the colour has stopped spreading before you add more colour.

5. Once the filter is covered in colour, leave to dry.

6. When dry, use the paper to cut out leaf shapes.

### Taking it forward

- Use the coffee filter leaves to create a window display.

- If you are using food colouring as opposed to liquid water colour, remember to water it down first.

### What's in it for the children?

The children will be exploring the concept of cause and effect, as well as investigating the unique properties of the filter paper and how it responds to liquid. There will be lots of opportunities to talk about colour and colour mixing, as well as developing their language and talking about aspects of autumn, colour and texture

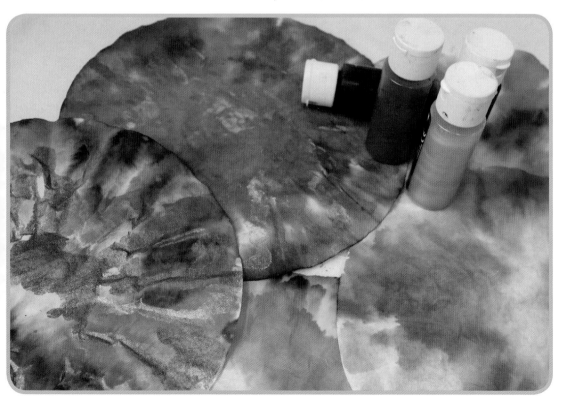

# Leaf globe

## What you need:

- Jam jar or plastic jar with a lid
- Twig
- Glue gun
- Water
- Autumn leaves
- Scissors
- Glitter (optional)

## What to do:

1. Find a twig that will fit inside the jar.
2. Using the glue gun, glue the twig to the inside of the lid of your jar.
3. Cut up the autumn leaves to make 'leaf confetti'.
4. Fill the jar with water.
5. Add your leaf confetti and any glitter or sequins.
6. Put the lid on your jar and tighten until it's secure.
7. Turn upside down and watch the leaves fall.

## Taking it forward

- Add different autumn resources to your jar such as sycamore keys, beech nuts etc.

## What's in it for the children?

This is a great talking point for children. It encourages them to talk about what they know about autumn, and also think about why and how leaves fall from the trees at this time of year.

# Window art

## What you need:

- Sticky backed plastic
- Leaves
- Sticky tack
- Masking tape
- Paint
- PVA glue
- Sponges

## What to do:

**1.** Cut the sticky backed plastic so that it is a suitable size for your artwork.

**2.** Use a little piece of masking tape in each corner to secure the sheet of sticky backed plastic to a flat surface. The paper side should be against the surface and the shiny side should face up.

**3.** Use sticky tack to position the leaves onto the sticky backed plastic.

**4.** Mix a teaspoon of PVA glue into the paint.

**5.** Using a sponge, apply the paint to the top of your leaves.

**6.** Leave to dry.

**7.** Remove the leaves and the sticky tack.

**8.** Peel off the paper backing and stick to a window.

### Taking it forward

- Use smaller and more complex leaf shapes to challenge children's physical dexterity.

### What's in it for the children?

The children are exploring the skill of printing and looking at relief printing. Once again, there are lots of opportunities for talk and exploration of colour and colour mixing.

### Top tip ★

Adding PVA to your paint will help it to adhere to the sticky backed plastic. You can always stick a second piece of plastic over your picture to protect the surface.

# Pumpkin moon sand

## What you need:

- Large bowl or container
- Four cups of play sand
- Two cups of cornflour
- Orange food colouring, liquid watercolours, or powdered paint
- Spices/flavouring such as cinnamon
- One to three cups of water

## What to do:

1. Add all of the dry ingredients to the container.
2. Add the colour and then the flavouring (if using).
3. Slowly stir in the water until you get the desired consistency.
4. Let the children experiment with the moon sand, enjoying its colour and texture.

### Taking it forward

- Add some pumpkin seeds for texture.
- Add some Halloween accessories like plastic spiders.

### What's in it for the children?

This is a great activity for a sensory experience. The moon sand has a unique texture and moulding it helps children to develop their gross and fine motor dexterity. Moon sand is a really open ended resource that can be interpreted by children in a variety of ways. It is great for imaginative play.

# Autumn popcorn

## What you need:

- Popcorn maker
- Popcorn kernels
- Food colouring in autumn colours or liquid water colour (if not for consumption)
- Paintbrush
- Small containers
- Paper, card or tray

## What to do:

1. Follow the instructions on your popcorn maker to produce a batch of popcorn.

2. Separate the popcorn into containers (one for each of the colours you are going to make).

3. Spread the popcorn out onto a piece of paper, card or in a tray.

4. Dip your paintbrush into the food colouring or liquid water colour.

5. Touch the popcorn lightly with the end of the brush and watch the colour 'bleed' into the pieces of popcorn.

### Taking it forward

- For a quicker process put the popcorn into a freezer bag with drops of colour and shake. Repeat the process until you have the colour you need.

- Use several colours on the same piece of popcorn.

- Thread pieces of popcorn together for an autumnal garland.

### What's in it for the children?

The children will have the opportunity to observe the change to the unpopped popcorn when heat is applied to it. They can also explore colour and colour mixing.

# Hot chocolate paint

## What you need:

- Bowl
- Shaving foam
- Powdered hot chocolate
- Brown paint or food colouring
- Spoon

## What to do:

1. Fill your bowl with shaving foam.
2. Slowly stir in some hot chocolate powder.
3. Add some brown paint or food colouring until you have got the desired colour.
4. Let the children have fun applying the chocolate paint to suitable surfaces!

### Taking it forward

- You can 'serve' this paint in mugs and provide a brush so that children can paint directly from the mug.

### What's in it for the children?

The paint is really smooth and easy to apply with both fingers and brushes. It also smells fantastic! Make sure you point out to the children that, even though it smells like hot chocolate, it is not a good idea to eat it!

# Puffy paint snowflakes

## What you need:

- Flour
- Water
- Squeezy bottle
- Microwave
- Cardboard
- Bowl
- Spoon

## What to do:

1. Mix an equal amount of flour and water in a bowl.
2. Stir the mixture until it is the consistency of pancake batter.
3. Pour the mixture into a squeezy bottle, such as a washing-up liquid bottle and shake.
4. Trace the shape of a snowflake onto a piece of card by gently squeezing the mixture out of the bottle.
5. Place the card into the microwave.
6. Microwave on full power for 30 seconds.

### Taking it forward

- You can sprinkle glitter onto your snowflake as soon as it comes out of the microwave.
- Once cool, you can cut around your snowflake design and hang from string or thread.

### What's in it for the children?

The children have the opportunity to observe how combining substances can change their consistency and also the effect that applying heat can have.

# Glass soap pictures

## What you need:

- **Small bars of soap** (or cut a large bar into smaller bars with a sharp knife)
- Mirrors
- Glass doors or windows

## What to do:

1. Cut the soap into small pieces.

2. Use the soap to draw directly onto the mirror or glass.

3. You can show the children pictures of ice/frost on glass (or show them the real thing) and ask them to use it as an inspiration for their work.

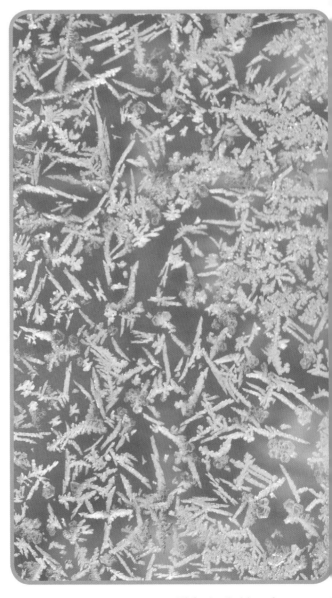

**Taking it forward**

- Using soaps with different scents will create a 'scented' picture.
- Wash away your artwork using warm water and a cloth.

**What's in it for the children?**

The children will experience the sensation of using soap on a smooth surface. They will also have the opportunity to consolidate their fine motor dexterity and mark making skills.

# Snowflake printing

## What you need:

- Fir tree branch
- White paint
- Tray or container
- Paper or card
- Scissors
- Glitter (optional)

## What to do:

1. Cut the end off your fir tree branch.
2. Pour some white paint into your tray or container.
3. Push the end of your fir tree branch into your paint.
4. Use the end of your branch to print onto your paper.
5. Sprinkle your paper with glitter whilst the paint is still wet.
6. Leave to dry.

### Taking it forward

- Use the same technique to print directly onto windows and doors.
- Use larger varieties of fir tree to produce bigger snowflakes.

### What's in it for the children?

Holding and printing with the fir tree is a great sensory experience for the children. It stimulates their sense of touch and sense of smell.

# Ice jewellery

## What you need:

- Ice cube tray
- Water
- Liquid water colour or food colouring
- Thread or string
- Glitter and sequins
- Freezer

## What to do:

1. Fill the ice cube tray with water.
2. Add liquid water colour or food colouring to each of the individual sections of the ice cube tray.
3. Take a length of thread or string and lay it across the ice cube tray. Ensure that a piece of the thread or string is immersed in each section of the tray.
4. Add glitter and sequins to each section of the tray.
5. Freeze overnight.
6. Turn out the ice cubes.
7. Join the ends of the thread or string to create your ice jewellery.

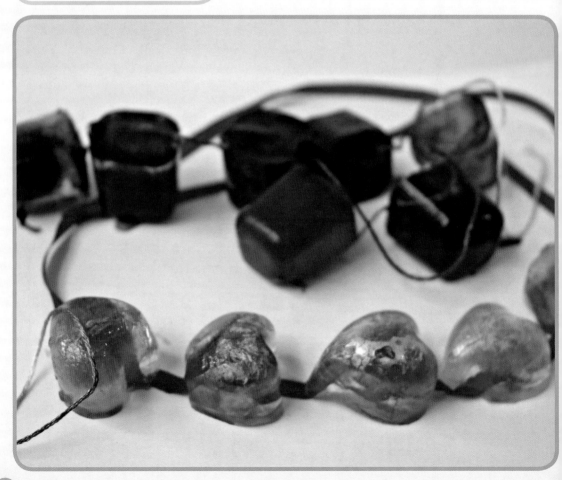

### Taking it forward

- Use ice cube trays with different shapes, such as stars or hearts.

- Create ice rings by bending a pipe cleaner and immersing the bend in your ice cube tray before freezing.

### What's in it for the children?

The children will observe how water changes from a liquid to a solid when it is frozen and then changes back to a liquid again when heated.

# Cinnamon snowflakes

## What you need:

- White tortillas
- Cinnamon
- Sugar
- Baking tray
- Melted butter
- Oven
- Scissors

## What to do:

1. Preheat the oven to 180 degrees.
2. Gently warm the tortillas so that they bend but don't crack.
3. Fold each tortilla in half, in half again and then once more.
4. Use scissors to cut shapes out of your folded tortilla, as if you were making a paper snowflake.
5. Unfold the tortilla snowflakes and brush with melted butter.
6. Sprinkle your tortilla with cinnamon and sugar.
7. Bake in the oven for five to ten minutes.
8. Cool and eat!

**Taking it forward**

- Try adding some edible glitter to your snowflake.
- Save all of the bites that you cut out of your tortilla. Apply the same process and bake separately for some 'snowflake bites'.

**What's in it for the children?**

The children are not only making themselves a treat to eat, but they are also exploring their cutting and baking skills.

# Potato head snowmen

## What you need:

- Snow!
- Modelling resources, such as googly eyes, wool, pipe cleaners and bottle tops

## What to do:

1. Use your hands to roll the snow into a potato sized ball.
2. Use the modelling resources to decorate your snowball.
3. Enjoy playing with your potato head snowman.

### Taking it forward

- Bring snow indoors in bowls or on a tray for an indoor modelling activity.
- Keep your models in the freezer and get them out later in the year!

### What's in it for the children?

This activity allows the children to create a small scale snowman that they can then use in their small world and imaginary play.

# Sandpaper and wool winter art

## What you need:

- **Pieces of cotton thread and wool** (various colours)
- **Sheets of sandpaper**
- **Scissors**
- **Hairspray**

**Taking it forward**

- Use wax crayons to give your picture some extra colour.

- Create a snow effect by snipping the end of white wool strands and pressing them into the sandpaper.

- You can create a much larger picture by using sticky backed plastic instead of sand paper. Peel off the back and create your own wool picture on the sticky side.

## What to do:

1. Cut the cotton and the wool into pieces of various lengths.

2. Create patterns and pictures on the sandpaper using the wool.

3. Use your fingers to move the cotton and wool around your picture.

4. Once you are happy with your picture, lightly press the wool and cotton to make sure that it sticks.

5. Lightly spray your picture with hairspray. This will help the thread and wool to stick.

**What's in it for the children?**

Using wool and thread can be a real challenge for children's fine motor dexterity.

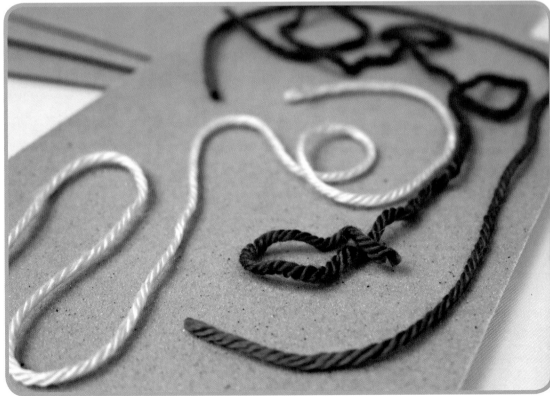

# Newspaper snowman

## What you need:

- Newspaper
- Masking tape
- Coloured card
- Woolly hat
- Scarf
- Twigs (optional)
- Glue

## What to do:

1. Scrunch up your newspaper to create two balls. Ensure one ball is slightly larger than the other.

2. Wrap the balls in a sheet of newspaper and secure it in place with masking tape.

3. Tape the smaller ball onto the top of the larger ball.

4. Using the coloured card, cut out some eyes, a carrot nose and a mouth.

5. Glue the eyes, nose and mouth to the smaller ball. This will be the head of the newspaper snowman.

6. Dress the snowman in a hat and scarf.

7. Glue the twigs into the body of your snowman to make arms.

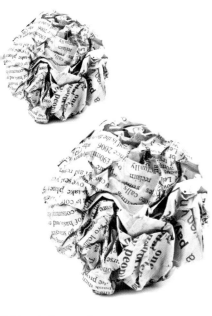

### Taking it forward

- You could paint the newspaper snowman white before adding the clothes and features.

- Wrap the newspaper balls in white paper if you don't want to paint your snowman.

### What's in it for the children?

This is a great activity to do indoors if it is too cold to go out but there isn't any snow. The children will be using their fine and gross motor dexterity skills when constructing their snowman.

# Ice cave

## What you need:

- Balloon
- Water
- Food colouring
- Freezer
- Scissors
- Small world figures and toys

## What to do:

1. Fill the balloon with water.
2. Add a few drops of food colouring to the water in the balloon and tie the top tightly.
3. Place the balloon in the freezer for four to five hours.
4. Once the balloon has begun to freeze, but is not completely frozen, take it out of the freezer.
5. Use the scissors to cut off the balloon over a sink, revealing a balloon shaped ice cube. Drain away any unfrozen water.
6. Use your balloon ice cave for small world play and exploration.

### Taking it forward

- Make multiple ice caves in different colours and stack them together to create an ice kingdom.
- Make your ice caves outdoors if the weather is cold enough. The children can experiment with water when they cut open their balloons.

### What's in it for the children?

The children will have the opportunity to observe how liquid changes state when it transforms from water into ice. They will also get a clear idea of how long that process takes.

# Snow ice cream

## What you need:

- Four cups of clean snow
- One cup of milk
- Quarter cup of sugar
- One teaspoon of vanilla essence
- Zip lock bag

## What to do:

1. Combine all of the ingredients in the zip lock bag.
2. Seal the bag.
3. Shake the bag to combine the ingredients so that they are the consistency of ice cream.
4. Open the bag and eat your snow ice cream!

### Taking it forward

- Add different flavours to your ice cream. Try adding hot chocolate powder or food essences, such as orange or strawberry.
- Turn your snack area into an ice cream parlour so that the children can engage in role play while they eat their snack!

### What's in it for the children?

The children will be able to see the effect that the snow has on the other ingredients in the bag. If they taste the snow before they mix in the other ingredients they will see how the milk, sugar and essence alter the flavour.

### Health & Safety

You need to be completely sure the snow is clean and fit for tasting. If you are aware of an imminent snow fall, you could put a bowl out to collect it and use that instead.

# frost paint

## What you need:

- Half cup of boiling water
- Half cup of Epsom salts

## What to do:

1. Mix the boiling water with the Epsom salts.
2. Leave the liquid to cool.
3. Paint over any picture with your frost paint to create a 'frosted' effect.

### Taking it forward

- Add some glitter into your mixture to give it added sparkle.

### What's in it for the children?

The children will be able to observe how the salt crystals dissolve in the hot water and then how they form again in a different way when the salt solution dries out.

### Health & Safety

An adult should handle the boiling water and only allow the children to use the mix when it has fully cooled.

# Snow toffee

## What you need:

- Snow
- One cup of maple syrup
- Quarter cup of butter
- Pan
- Cooker

## What to do:

1. Put your maple syrup into a pan.
2. Bring the syrup to a slow boil **(adult only)**.
3. Once boiling, carefully take the pan off the heat.
4. Take the pan outside and pour the contents into the snow **(adult only)**.
5. Watch the syrup cool and solidify to form toffee.
6. Pick the toffee out of the snow and eat.

### Taking it forward

- If you want perfect snow toffee, use a baking thermometer and make sure that your maple syrup reaches 230 degrees before you pour it into the snow.

### What's in it for the children?

Apart from a really tasty treat, the children get to see the way that temperature alters the state and consistency of a substance.

 **Health & Safety**

An adult should handle the heating process. You need to be completely sure the snow is clean and fit for tasting. If you are aware of an imminent snow fall, you could put a bowl out to collect it and use that instead.